ISBN 978-1-333-63358-5
PIBN 10528973

1 MONTH OF
FREE
READING

at
www.ForgottenBooks.com

By purchasing this book you are eligible for one month membership to ForgottenBooks.com, giving you unlimited access to our entire collection of over 700,000 titles via our web site and mobile apps.

To claim your free month visit:
www.forgottenbooks.com/free528973

English
Français
Deutsche
Italiano
Español
Português

www.forgottenbooks.com

Mythology Photography **Fiction**
Fishing Christianity **Art** Cooking
Essays Buddhism Freemasonry
Medicine **Biology** Music **Ancient
Egypt** Evolution Carpentry Physics
Dance Geology **Mathematics** Fitness
Shakespeare **Folklore** Yoga Marketing
Confidence Immortality Biographies
Poetry **Psychology** Witchcraft
Electronics Chemistry History **Law**
Accounting **Philosophy** Anthropology
Alchemy Drama Quantum Mechanics
Atheism Sexual Health **Ancient History**
Entrepreneurship Languages Sport
Paleontology Needlework Islam
Metaphysics Investment Archaeology
Parenting Statistics Criminology
Motivational

IRISH POEMS. BY
KATHARINE TYNAN

SECOND IMPRESSION

LONDON : SIDGWICK & JACKSON, LTD.
ADAM STREET, ADELPHI   MCMXIV

To

THE FIRST GENTLEMAN IN IRELAND AND
THE MOST GRACIOUS

CONTENTS

8 CONTENTS

PAGE

CONTENTS

THE COMING BACK

To the Lord MacDonnell

WHEN I came back to Ireland the leaves on the tree,
The birds on the branches would keep reminding me,
With, *don't you remember?* and *could you forget?*
Till I'm living and walking in the old times yet.

The wind from the mountains it blows fresh and strong:
Ah, don't you remember? is still the wind's song.
With, *don't you remember?* and *could you forget?*
As I went out a-walking 'twas the dead that I met.

There's a road runs to Wicklow : it goes past the door.
The dust of it's holy for feet it once bore.
They've all travelled Westward where the sun doesn't
    set.
Ah, don't you remember? and *could you forget?*

The blackbird he's mocking from the apple-bough :
Sure why would you trouble to be coming now
When them that sore missed you is past fear and fret?
Ah, don't you remember? and *could you forget?*

There's not a flower in Ireland, there isn't a hill,
Nor yet a breath of the Four Winds but keeps reminding
    still,
Till my poor heart is troubled and my eyes are wet
For *don't you remember?* and *could you forget?*

EPIPHANY

To Rudolph Mary John O'Riordan

THE Kings have brought Him ambergris,
The Babe, whose one delight it is
    To creep and nest
In the warm snows of Mother's breast.

The Kings have brought Him frankincense,
Who hath no need, this Innocence,
    Of aught beside
His Mother's milk in a full tide.

O'er Mother's breast His fingers go,
Constraining that sweet stream to flow,
    So soft and small,
To whom that milky world is all.

The Kings have brought Him gold and myrrh,
This new-born thing whose Heaven's in her ;
    To make His bed
In the sweet place from which He fed.

Myrrh, spikenard, such precious things,
The Kings have brought the King of Kings,
    Who, dronken-deep,
Falls like a full-fed lamb asleep.

THE HOUSE OF THE LORD

To the Lord Kilbracken

I WOULD choose to be a doorkeeper
  In the House of the Lord
Rather than lords and ladies
  In satin on the sward.
To draw the bolts for the white souls
  Would be my rich reward :
And I the happy doorkeeper
  To the House of the Lord.

Of all troop in not one comes out
  From the House of the Lord,
Those who have won from sin and death,
  From age and grief abhorred.
There is more room within its courts
  Than palaces afford ;
So great it is and spacious
  In the House of the Lord.

They come with shining faces
  To the House of the Lord ;
The broken hearts and weary
  That life has racked and scored :

They come hurrying and singing
    To sit down at His board,
They are young and they are joyful
    In the House of the Lord.

There are lilies and daisies
    In the House of the Lord.
The lover finds his lover
    With a long, long regard.
The mothers find the children,
    Strayed from their watch and ward.
O the meetings and the greetings
    In the House of the Lord !

I would be a humble doorkeeper
    In the House of the Lord,
Where the courts are white and shining
    In the Light of the Word.
When the saved souls come trooping
    For the gates to be unbarred,
O blessed is the doorkeeper
    In the House of the Lord !

THE MOUNTAINS

To my Father

I HEARD them talk of the mountains,
   The kind and innocent folk:
Something troubled the fountains
   The grief in my heart awoke.

My heart was a heart that broke;
   Something troubled the fountains;
The grief in my heart awoke
   When they talked of the mountains.

Over the mountain blue,
   By the fields and the winding boreen,
I walked and I talked with you
   In days that are over, asthoreen.

We walked together, asthoreen,
   When the blackbird sang in the dew;
As we talked by the fields and the boreen
   My heart was a bird that flew.

2

Now it is heavy as lead,
  No matter how fine the weather;
It falls like a thing stone-dead
  That once was light as a feather.

We walked and we talked together,
  And pleasant the things we said :
The larks sprang out of the heather.
  Och, many's the tear I've shed !

The kind and innocent people
  Discourse of the mountains still.
I think of a low grey steeple
  And the graves lying under the hill.

Ochone—these Summers are chill !
  They were meaning nothing, the people.
My heart went crying its fill
  For a new grave under the steeple.

ANY WIFE

NOBODY knows but you and I, my dear,
And the stars, the spies of God, that lean and peer,
Those nights when you and I in a narrow strait
Were under the whips of God and desolate.
In extreme pain, in uttermost agony.
We bore the cross for each other, you and I,
When, through the darkest hour, the night of dread,
I suffered and you supported my head.

Ties that bind us together for life and death,
Oh, hard-set fight in the darkness, shuddering breath,
Because a man can only bear as he may,
And find no tears for easing, the woman's way.
Anguish of pity, sharp in the heart like a sword :
Dost Thou not know, O Lord ?   Thou knowest, Lord,
What we endured for each other : our wounds were red
When he suffered and I supported his head.

Grief that binds us closer than smile or kiss,
Into the pang God slips the exquisite bliss.

You were my angel and I your angel, as he,
The angel, comforted Christ in His agony,
Lifting Him up from the earth that His blood made **wet,**
Pillowing the holy head, dabbled in sweat.
Thou **who** wert under the scourges knowest **to** prove
Love by its pangs, love that endures for love.

THE LITTLE HOUSE

To Alice Meynell

I WILL have a little house
  When the children are flown.
The feel of a big house
  Would be cold as a stone ;
A house full of emptiness
  And we two alone.

But in a little house
  We could creep to the blaze ;
We could warm our old hearts
  With the thought of old days ;
Him and me together
  When the firelight plays.

There would hardly be room
  For the ghosts to come in :
Ghosts of the little children
  Who made a merry din,
Long ago and long ago
  When I was a queen.

I will have a little garden
  Big enough for two,
Where we can walk together
  When the skies are blue,
Talking the good days over
  And how fast they flew.

The littlest house and garden
  For him and me just.
And all the sweet times we had
  Withered to dust.
A big house would break my heart
  For the children lost.

THE MIST THAT'S OVER IRELAND

To Ronald Ross

THERE'S a mist that's over Ireland where the blackbird
    calls,
And when you come it's risin' and when you go it falls.
It's made of green and silver and the rain and dew,
And the finest sun is over it you ever knew.

Och, sure it isn't mist at all, except a mist o' tears,
A haze of love and longin' for the happy years,
When myself that's old and fretted now and colder than
    the stone
Was young in golden Ireland with the friends long gone.

The mist is like a curtain that the wind'll blow
And lift a little wisp of it till you see below
The shiningest country ever was of hills and streams,
And the people do be haunting you in lonesome dreams.

The people do be in the mist, their like's hard to
    find,
Their faces full of welcome and their smile soft and
    kind.
It was little I was thinkin' in the days that ran away
How I'd sit and break my heart for them one weary day.

It isn't fields and mountains and it isn't streams and
    trees,
Though all o' them is in the mist, nor hummin' of the
    bees,
Nor yet the thrush and blackbird could vex me as I stand
And look the way of Ireland with my head in my hand.

'Tis little that we value them, when we're gay and
    young ;
We think we'll have them with us, our whole lives long.
We never know the good we have till constant friends
    depart
And leave us just with half a life and half a heart.

There's a gold mist over Ireland that for me will never
    rise,
And some is walkin' in it was the light of my eyes.

They're never old and troubled now, and never sick and
    sad.
The days we had together were the best I had.

Please God, some day that's comin', when the dread of
    death 's past,
And I take the lonesome valley we all must take at last,
I'll sight the hills of Heaven and the people in white,
And you, and you, among them was my heart's delight.

The mist that's over Ireland will be blowin' in my face;
I'll reach the other side of it to the well-remembered
    place,
And I'll not be lookin' backward like a lonesome ghost
From the mist that's over Ireland and the friends I lost.

THE MEETING

To Ada Tyrrell

As I went through the ancient town,
  Long lost and found once more,
Oh, who is this in a green gown
  I knew so well of yore ?

Veils of enchantment hid the place,
  Hung every street and square ::
I felt the sea-wind in my face
  And ruffling in my hair.

Oh town I loved so well and lost,
  And find again with tears,
Your streets hold many a darling ghost
  And all the vanished years !

My heart went singing a low song,
  Glad to be home again.
But who is this comes blithe and young,
  Not feared of life but fain ?

Oh, who is this comes cold as stone
  To my quick cry and call ?
Of all the faces loved and flown
  I knew her best of all.

"Stay, you are . . ." Is she deaf and blind
  Or hath she quite forgot ?
What chill is in the sun, the wind,
  Because she knows me not ?

As I went down—my eyes were wet—
  Eager and stepping fast
That was my own sweet youth I met
  Who knew me not and passed.

FEBRUARY IN ·LONDON

To A. H. Bullen

THE grey streets of London are sweeter than the rose,
The grey streets of London when the West Wind blows.
The wild wind, the fresh wind, brings home the Spring
    again
And I turn my face to meet her in the softest rain.

The tired folk and busy they put their cares away
With : Never mind to-morrow since life is good to-day.
They are wondering what ails them, the West Wind
    blows so sweet,
With a flash of green and silver in the saddest street.

There's dappled sky above us if the smoke would let
    us see.
In dingy squares and crescents there's a thrush upon
    the tree.
The rain like little fingers comes with a soft surprise
And is smoothing out the wrinkles round the weary eyes.

The rain and the West Wind that set the flowers to start
They wash the grime from off the soul, the grief from
the heart.
And who would you be meeting as you walk the murky
town
But Spring that's like a daffodil in a golden gown ?

The girls beside the pavements they carry golden store
Of wallflowers and hyacinths and violets galore.
The soft speech of Limerick I heard as I went by
And the blue eyes of Ireland were like a glint of sky.

The West Wind is blowing on people stepping light.
They wonder what is on them ; they feel so queer and
bright.
The softest rain is falling, and while the West Wind blows
The grey streets of London are sweeter than the rose.

LULLABY

AFTER THE RUSSIAN

To Katharine Ross

God the Father gave thee me,
Jesus Christ presented thee.

Mary that's without a stain
Brought thee to my window-pane,

Nursing thee, so little and good,
Under her hair and her blue hood.

" Olga," said the blessed one,
" Take thou him and call him John.

Call him, from the Baptist, John,
And him who was my second son."

Blessed Mary tossed me thee
As a young rose from a young tree.

" For all he is so soft and small
He will be thy man and tall."

Said Mother Mary : " Olga, take him ;
With thy milky bosom slake him.

See he sleeps when he is fed
Lest he cry uncomforted."

Mary Mother in Heaven's joy
Took so great thought for my boy.

" When thou goest to the well
Linger not to gossip and tell.

When thou goest to the shop
Loiter not lest he wake up,

And peace in Heaven be undone
Because a child cries all alone."

Sleep now, little John, that playest.
Christ be with thee where thou strayest

In the most sweet fields of sleep
Where He leads His lambs and sheep.

When the time comes thou shalt rise
With loveliest dreams in quiet eyes.

Sleep steals at even-fall
Along the bench, beside the wall.

While fade in dreams father and mother
Sleep and weariness kiss each other.

Drowsiness in sleepy streams
Falls like rain or the moonbeams.

Sleep says : " Give me the child " :
Hushes thee at her breast so mild.

" Sleep," she breathes, " lie still and warm,
Little John, in the bend o' my arm."

Drowsiness at the small ear
Whispers, " I am sleepy, dear."

Drowsiness in a grey veil
And Sleep like the moon pale

Kneel beside thy cradle stirred ;
And the bee's asleep and the bird.

The angels keeping watch
By the pane, lifting the latch,

Ask if thou sleepest sweet—
Little eyes, little hands, little feet.

REPROACH

To Father Russell

WHEN I came back to Ireland 'twas little I knew
   The sorrow was waiting for me in the good year's
      gloam.
You who were always tender, was it kind of you
   To be up and going your lonesome road and I barely
      come ?

It was not like you, O kindest one, to go in such haste !
   Barely to say " You are welcome home " and then
      to be gone.
A little glance and a word of love, and you stepping fast
Over the brink of the Autumn world after the sun.

If I had known, O kindest one, and I full of joy !
   How soon my land would be empty of you, losing
      your light,
Could I have come, singing my songs, like a girl or a boy,
   And the black desolation beyond and the wintry
      night ?

That was the one unkindness you showed me, my dear ;
   And I so glad of the mountains and fields and the
      friends of old :
For you to be turning your back on me in my wonderful
      year,
   Taking the light and comfort with you, leaving me
      cold,

THE WOUNDS

To Lady Grosvenor

God's Son had Wounds Five
To save men's souls alive.

Five Wounds, five Joys, Heartsease,
That spring for man's release.

The First Wound it pierced and struck
The hand that blessed and broke.

The Second stabbed with cruel smart
The hand was next His heart.

Of the Third Wound what shall be said
Wherewith His side was red ?

An Heavenly House, a Rosy Ark
To house men from the dark.

The Fourth and Fifth His feet did keep
That followed after His sheep

Nailed to the Cross lest they should press
On their high business.

The Wounds of Love they throbbed and bled ;
In Heaven they are not stayed.

In Heaven they are red roses five
That save men's souls alive.

Five roses on a heavenly tree
And Christ's men shall go free.

Five roses, crimson-dyed
In His hands, in His feet, in His side.

Five roses set between
God's anger and man's sin.

THE CONFLICT

To Father Edmund Lester, S.J.

O MARY, Queen, and God's Mother,
    In Jesu's Name I pray.
Thy heart had seven sad swords, Mother,
    The which was thy Son's stay.
Now that my little son must fight
    And dragons overthrow;
O Mother of the World's Delight,
    Arm him before he go.

For all thy seven-fold wounds, Mother,
    And for thy joys full-five,
Keep him within thy bounds, Mother,
    And save his soul alive.
For thy Son's sake who could not sin
    Send Michael to his aid,
That ere the deadly jousts begin
    My son be not dismayed.

Yea, make him thine own knight, Mother,
    With sword of living flame.

His banners all of white, Mother,
  To bear thy spotless name.
O set thy lilies on his shield,
  The which the beast must dread.
Sit thou above the tourney-field
  To crown the victor's head.

But if he faint and fall, Mother,
  Be thou the first to run.
And in the sight of all, Mother,
  Lift him, my little son.
Yea, let his last sight be of thee,
  His fight be not in vain,
His last shout be of victory
  Although himself be slain.

THE PHILOSOPHER
To John O'Mahony

Whᴇɴ I came back to Ireland from a foreign shore,
The stress of money-gettin' had made me sick and sore.
Och, foolishness of people, when no man needs to have,
And be he lord or peasant, but at last a grave.

Their land was thick with churches : aye, many spires
     on spires.
The people, lookin' sorry, in cities and in shires,
Were readin' of their Bibles : one text they missed, be
     sure :
" The poor are always with you ! "   Ah, God help the
     poor !

They haven't too much honour over there, I find.
The country where small money is is better to my mind.
They don't be dramin' money and a man has got the
     time
To look at seas and mountains and to turn a rhyme.

They're neighbourly in Ireland, and if they've little store
They'd share it with a neighbour and there's still the
     open door.

For him that turns the poor away may turn away unfed
The very Son of God Himself as He begs for bread.

They won't be makin' money of the water and the land.
Plase God they'll learn no stintin', but keep the open
    hand,
And what they lose they're savin' and what they give
    they hold.
Ah, God help the foolish people with the yellow gold !

There's never any hurry here : there's always time to
    say
" God save you kindly ! " as we go, and pass the time
    of day ;
To smoke a pipe beside the fire, or may be in the sun,
And be holdin' kind discourses of the friends that's gone.

The sun upon your shoulders will warm you through
    and through ;
And souls are more than bodies in the place we're travel-
    lin' to.
Och, take a sate, my travelled man, the sunny side the
    ditch,
And be lavin' money-makin' to the foolish rich !

SHANGANAGH

To Mrs. Rowan Hamilton

LAUGHS the darling river, hurrying, dancing onward.
  Sorrow she knows of maybe, the bird's or the bee's,
Or some butterfly weary, its wings dropped downward,
  Caught in a swirling eddy, drowned in her seas.

Maybe the hedge-sparrow, maybe the starling,
  Hath lost here some sweet thing of its downy brood.
Never lamb or kid or any woman's darling
  Hath she thought of drowning in her wildest mood.

From her golden bed, set with many a jewel,
  No white face starts upward, piteous to the skies;
None hath sought here rest from sweet love grown cruel,
  Hiding a sad secret from the mocking eyes.

Bare she lies to Heaven 'mid her mints and cresses,
  Innocent of evil as a lamb or a child.
The sun and stars love her and the wind caresses,
  Ruffling her little waters so soft and wild.

As she slips away by a mossy boulder
   The child dips a rosy foot where she foams and swirls,
Shows her a darling cheek and a dimpled shoulder,
   Laughs to see his face in her, set in its curls.

Here the lamb drinks deep without fear or fretting :
   There are no wolves, no danger, for child or lamb ;
Only the Angels of God that are never forgetting
   Keep the child for his mother, the lamb for his dam.

THE WINTER GARDEN

To Lady Harrel

THE Winter Garden lies at rest,
The clay upon her brows and breast,
The winding sheet drawn to her chin,
Her eyes blue the lids within.

The Winter Garden grieved and pined,
Alone, out in the rain and wind,
Until she fell asleep, so pure
A quiet sleeper, still, demure.

They heaped her shroud with rose and myrtle.
Lilies, carnations strewed her kirtle ;
Her kirtle of the green is on
Under the cere-cloth, straight and wan.

Sleeping she hath within her arms
The wild songs and the soft charms.
The butterfly by her is laid,
The bee streaked in her chilly bed.

A day will come, a day and hour
Of a wild hope and a warm shower ;
And a voice crying in bush and brake :
" The maid sleepeth : Daughter, awake."

The Winter Garden then will rise,
Cast the clay from mouth and eyes ;
Her eyes will be the eyes of a bride,
The King's Daughter be glorified.

In her green kirtle she will show,
Scattering blossoms she will go :
She shall trip it on a green hill,
With the wind-flower and the daffodil.

Alone—withouten leaf or bud,
What wild dreams stir in her blood ?
Under her hood what dream of mirth
Of a new Heaven and a new earth ?

THE OLD MAGIC

To G. W., who sped me

As I go down from Dalkey and by Killiney Strand
  There's something queer about the world: it's all so
    clean and new!
As though this very minute God put it from His hand
  And soft airs of Paradise blew.

So fresh it was and shining, the sapphire seas and skies,
  The silver-misted mountains and the gorse newly gold.
The big brown lovely headland troubles my heart and
    eyes,
  Till 'tis growing young I am, not old.

I wonder will it stay so, the years I have to live.
  With fairy people spreading their spells on sea and
    hill;
Their webs as fine as gossamer that fairy spinners weave;
  And the old enchantment work its will.

'Twas worth the twenty years away to see it as I see.
  For them that sees it every day's too used to it to
  mind.
I wonder how I stayed so long and Ireland calling me,
  And her breast so warm and kind.

THE MAKER

To Maude Egerton King

GOD made the country,
    Man made the town.
God clad the country
    In a green gown.

Clad her in kirtle
    Of the green silk.
God made the country
    Of honey and milk.

Poor folk from Eden
    Driven away,
God made the country
    For a holiday.

God gave the country
    A flower, a bird,
To comfort His children
    For the flaming sword.

For easing and pleasing
  He made a tree,
Many a sweet rivulet,
  Dew and the bee.

God made the country,
  Man made the town.
Is not God a maker
  Of great renown ?

THE STRONG FIGHT

To the Lady Glenconner for Heartsease

I BUILD a strong tower for the children, the children;
  With moat and portcullis I keep it still.
The foe clangs without but within it the children
  Sleep soundly and sweetly till cock-crow shrill.

I wage a Holy War for the children, the children ;
  My hand against the world that they may live.
I am cunning and crafty as the fox for her children,
  Wise as the serpent lest the children grieve.

I build a warm fire for the children, the children.
  To my tower oft beleaguered allies I call ;
They shine like the sun to the eyes of the children ;
  God's men-at-arms keep us by gate and wall.

I leave in safe keeping the children, the children.
  Down to the cities my way I take,
Past the walls and the sentry, alert for the children,
  I creep in the shadows for the children's sake.

I gather rich stores for the children, the children,
   The lowing of oxen is heard as I come :
I carry the sheaves in my arms for the children.
   Oh, sweet on the hill-top the lights of home.

Unless the Lord build it, the house for the children,
   Unless He be with me my labour's vain.
He has thought it and planned it, the fold for the
    children,
   Where the lambs be folded without fear or stain.

I fight the holy fight for the children, the children,
   The sons of God glorious sit down at my board.
Though the foes hem us in, shall I fear for the children,
   Fighting the strong fight in the Name of the Lord?

WIND IN THE WIRES

To Hester Sigerson

THE south-west wind among the wires
  Plays tunes I knew of old.
There's a blue sky above the spires,
  A blue sky and a gold.

His fingers move among the strings,
  He plays the whole day long
On his Æolian harp the things
  I knew when I was young.

What magic mist enchants my sight,
  That I would rise and go
With an uplifted heart and light
  The paths I used to know ?

They are all out, the lights, the fires,
  And under wind and rain
The wind among the telegraph-wires
  Wakes the old griefs in vain.

THE GREEN RIBBON

To My God-Child Olivia

ALL around my hat I will wear the green ribbon, O.
All round my hat for a year and a day ;
And if anybody asks me why do I wear it
I'll say that my true love is far, far away.

For green is the colour of the weeping willow, O,
And green is the colour for her that is true ;
Tell my love if he come not I die of my sorrow, O,
And shall sleep deep, forgetting the pangs I knew.

I shall say : " My sweet mother, make my bride-clothes
ready, O,"
I shall say : " Little sister, weep not for me,
But clothe me in silver like a beauteous lady, O,
And hide not my face lest he come and see."

Six gentle knights to the grave will carry me,
The maids shall strew violets my face above,
They will say : " She was constant," and weep as they
bury me,
Saying : " Here is a true maid who died of love."

O what have I to do with life and with living, O !
    If he should come not I shall not know.
I shall sleep on so sweetly, done with care and grieving,
      O,
    Alone in my bride-bed the moulds below.

List, ye grave pilgrims, who journey to Walsingham,
    Say if you meet him that his love lies sick—
Sore sick with loving and will soon be dying, O ;
    If he would save her that he travel quick.

All around my hat now I wear the green ribbon, O,
    So have I worn it a year and above ;
Say if he come not he will find me sleeping, O ;
    With a stone at my head that I died of love.

THE EXILE

To Frank Mathew

THERE are thrushes and finches in an English coppice.
　All the May night the nightingales are never still.
My heart turns and tosses on its bed of poppies,
　Desolate for the blackbird by an Irish hill.

Sweet are the English fields, dappled with blossom,
　The fine stacks of hay and corn are up to the eaves.
Sure, why would it trouble me, the heart in my bosom
　For a lone field in Ireland where the peewit grieves ?

Ordered and pleasant is an English garden ;
　In the happy orchards the fruit hangs red.
Still through the scented night my heart knew its
　　burden
　And through the golden day ; if naught was said.

Lovely the homesteads in an English country,
　Neither change nor ruin there as time goes by.
In a bower of roses, my heart keeping sentry
　Cried for my own country with a lonesome cry.

THE LEPER

NOT white and shining like an ardent flame,
   Not like Thy Mother and the Saints in bliss,
But white from head to foot I bear my blame,
     White as the leper is.

Unclean ! unclean ! But Thou canst make me clean ;
   Yet if Thou cleanse me, Lord, see that I be
Like that one grateful leper of the ten
     Who ran back praising Thee.

But if I must forget, take back Thy word ;
   Be I unclean again but not ingrate.
Before I shall forget Thee, keep me, Lord,
     A sick man at Thy gate.

COMPENSATION

To Mr. Justice Ross

'Twas worth the years of exile just to recapture
  The old delight, the wild bliss of coming back.
I can praise God that I have tasted the rapture
  Before the night darkened upon my track.

Nigh on twenty years in a foreign city,
  And the best hour that hour in fog and rain,
Going home, and my heart singing its ditty
  In time to the creaking screw and the throbbing train.

Oh, the yellow streets and the poor sad people
  Trudging to their task in a pallid gloom
Below the black house-walls, under spire and steeple,
  And I for the sun at last and going home !

Sorry I was for them that weren't going,
  As though I travelled to lands where no man
    grieves.
My love she is, my heart's delight, and her West Wind
    blowing,
  And I coming home to her, carrying my sheaves !

GRANUAILE

To Miriam Alexander

THE green, oh the green, is the colour of the true.
And when the Winter's over what shall I do
But leave the town behind with the streets in dust and
     mire
And be stepping gladly Westward to my heart's desire ?

Far to the Westward my love doth reside,
Her knees are to her forehead at coming of night-tide.
By the shores of the ocean she prays for relief,
That the High King of Heaven may ease her of her grief.

To the High King's Son as a bride she is dear ;
She followed His sad fortunes through many a bitter
     year ;
With stripes she was scourgèd, and barefoot and poor,
Whom the King's Son delighted in, was driven from the
     door.

The King's Son hath dressed her in green of the sea.
Her beauty shall be lifted as high as His Tree.
Set on a high throne 'twixt the deep and the deep,
She shall call home her children as He calls His sheep.

Oh, when the Winter's over what shall I do
But follow and find her, the dear one and the true.
I am crying my lone in the mirk and the rain,
That the High-King of Heaven may bring me home
    again.

THE ROOM

To Ethel Brayden

THIS is my best hour of all,
When the quiet evenfall
Darkening over hill and plain
Brings the children home again.

Garnished is the room and sweet,
And the shaded lamp is lit.
To the rosy firelight gather
Three little folk from wind and weather.

All my birds have fluttered home
To the nest in the warm gloam.
And one roof-tree covers over
All I love and me the lover.

In the night what foes may lurk,
Evil shapes in the thick dark!
But the children warm and living
Know no sin and fear no grieving.

Three dear heads bent o'er their books,
And what need of shepherd's crooks ?
And what fear that lambs go straying
Folded in with love and praying ?

Three dear children will lie warm,
Safe from midnight and the storm ;
With an angel by them keeping
Guard lest aught disturb their sleeping.

Underneath my roof-tree groweth
Herb of grace, and Heartsease bloweth,
Pleasant places and a spring
For the children's comforting.

There shall come an evenfall
When no roof-tree covers all,
When the room shall be bereaven
And the mother of her Heaven.

In that day how sweet will rise
Visions of lost Paradise,
When one warm room held all treasure,
All delight in its scant measure.

THE TREE

To Wilfrid Meynell

WHEN that man was cast away
   Out of Eden for his sin,
God put by His wrath to say :
   " Now his sad time shall begin ;

My poor creature, made to walk
   By Me under forest trees,
Made to walk with Me and talk
   When the evening brings much ease :

Since a tree hath him undone,
   My poor creature that I planned,
By a Tree he shall be won,
   Given again into My Hand."

God took up a seed of life,
   Planted it in tear-wet earth :
" My poor Adam and his wife
   Shall have shade and quiet mirth.

This, My tree shall grow and grow
 Till its branches fill the air ;
Not my groves of Heaven may show
 Princely fruit as this shall bear.

Hanging head and knees, alack,
 This shall bear a noble Flower,
And My Tree will give Me back
 What I lost by Eden bower."

REPARATION

To Pamela

FOR that one angry word I spoke,
　　And for her wild surprise,
Through the long night, the still night,
　　I watch with sleepless eyes.

In the lone hour, the dark hour
　　Come back her grief and pain,
Again, her great and frightened eyes,
　　Her tears that ran like rain.

Then she was in my arms again,
　　Weeping against my breast :
In the grey house, the dim house
　　It will not let me rest.

For that one wrong I did, O child
　　Quick to forgive, forget,
In the dim light, the owl's light,
　　'Tis I remember yet.

THE GREAT ADVENTURE

To Ian Grant, R.N.

THE sailor now is safe at home.
  Amid the fields he sighs
For salt-sweet of the driven foam
  Upon his lips and eyes.

For now he takes his voyages
  Around his room and goes
Far as the corner where the bees
  Hum in the guelder rose.

A belt of woodland hems him in,
  Mid miles of trees he craves
For one clear sweep of the winds keen
  Over a world of waves.

No more he'll hear the great winds roar.
  He shall lie snug and warm,
Who roamed the world from Labrador
  Down to the Cape of Storm.

Beside his bed, idle at last
   His chart, his compass liè :
But he has seas untravelled, vast,
   And a chart to sail them by.

He takes his Bible in his hands—
   What gates are opening wide
To wonderful seas, untrodden lands,
   With Christ Himself for guide ?

He hears again the plash of oars ;
   A boat's beside the quay :
Like the great captains he adores
   He sails and sails away.

His seas are strewn with moon and stars ;
   The land he sails to find
Welcomes the veteran from Christ's wars
   Sped on a favouring wind.

Who loved o'er mortal seas to range,—
   But there's an end of all—
He sails the seas will never change
   With Christ for Admiral.

O what are ships of armour bright
   That lurking foes undo
To the winged ships are in his sight
   Manned by a heaven-bound crew ?

(There is one verse he will not read—
   His glasses aye are dim—
If there were no more sea indeed
   What lonesome heaven for him !)

His old head droops upon his breast,
   His eyes scarce see the page.
His last adventure and his best
   Falls to his weary age.

THE QUIET HOUSE

To Nora

'TIS very quiet in the house
    Without the turbulent little flock.
The sweet hours, quiet as a mouse,
    Steal slowly round the ticking clock.
We gather honey while we may
When children are at school all day.

So peaceful with the song of birds,
    The water lapping on the shore ;
But evening brings the flocks and herds
    And happy children home once more.
Blessed the hour in sun or rain
That brings the children home again.

'Tis very quiet in the house
    Where children come not home at all.
The day goes stiller than a mouse ;
    Gulls and the sea-winds cry and call :
And two old shadows by the flame
Talk of the days when children came.

Oh, when the children are away,
   The house is very still and sweet.
But if no evening, gold or grey,
   Brought the quick kiss, the flying **feet,**
Heavily would the silence press
The loneliness, the loneliness !

KILLINEY BAY

To Murrough O'Brien

HERE'S quietness for all who come,
   Rest for the weary heart and head,
A fragrant chamber, a hid room
   With downiest pillows, softest bed.

The lucent sky, amber and azure,
   The sea, a glittering shield of light,
And glory poured withouten measure,
   Flooding to starlight and the night.

Mountain on mountain : spear on spear :
   Brown hills that fold the singing streams.
(How many a day, how many a year
   I had the mountains but in dreams !)

A Spirit at dawns and evenfalls
   Glides by, her finger on her lip !
Yet there is sound : the blackbird calls,
   The poising sea-birds scream and dip.

The thin hill coppice, wild with starlings,
  Runs like a babbling stream in noise,
Where bridegrooms chatter to their darlings
  Of house-building and nuptial joys.

The sea breaks with a lapping soft,
  Lulling to quiet deeper still.
O silence of the sky aloft
  And silence of the heavenly hill!

Who would have quietness and rest,
  Peace for the heavy heart and head,
Come and be gathered to a breast,
  A quiet chamber, a soft bed!

THE COMMON

To Mary Blackwell

THERE are glades of gold on the Common, the Common
    now,
    Pillars and arches of the shining gold.
Here's a peace, a forgetting, for tired man and woman
    now,
    Fires to warm the heart at and the senses cold.

I've something to say of this Common—O wild and dear!
    She hath so many beauties as I could not tell.
She hath a tricksy spirit : listen, incline your ear :
    She lays all her lovers under fairy spell.

She has hills, she has hollows, she has gorse and bracken
    too,
    Wild winding pathways and secret groves.
Honey of the pinewood and sweets untaken too,
    Whispers and sighings for the heart that loves.

She's a fairy, a witch, oh gamesome, the shining one!
    She changes her face still 'twixt the night and day ;

" Why, here's a new glade now," I cry ; the designing
    one
  Laughs 'twixt the tree-trunks in the old wild way.

Over the Common I'm roaming and roaming then,
  By the secret pathway through bowers of leaves,
Know all her sweets by heart, the sweet that's coming
    then,
  Think I know it surely, but the witch deceives.

I cry to her face then : " You shall not deceive me,
  Wearing a new wile 'twixt day and gloam.
For all the disguises your fairy webs weave me
  I know the eyes under the hood.   Oh, witch, I come."

Up hill, down hollow, she flies and eludes me,
  Still from the shadow of trees her laughter rings.
With the old dear graces she holds and deludes me,
  But she's a witch too and a bird on wings.

I will say never more, where she mocks to hear it,
  " These are new heavens : I was never here."
She lays the spell on my eyes, the tricksy spirit
  Lays the spell on my heart, this Dryad dear.

THE CHILDREN'S WAY

To Sissie

THE children bear our froward mood,
  Patient, enduring still.
Our anger like a heat in the blood
  That strikes with little skill.

Because our way is choked with tares
  And fears beset our sleep ;
Because we weary Heaven with prayers
  Lest that the children weep.

The children must be warmed and fed,
  The children most adored :
Give them this day their daily bread !
  What of to-morrow, Lord ?

Therefore we strike them at their play
  And grieve their hearts and chill :
O Lord, be patient with the clay
  Thou'st moulded to Thy will.

See, Lord, the children understand !
  Loyal and piteous
They take the wounding from Love's hand.
  See, Lord,—they bear with us.

THE ASS SPEAKS

To Louise Imogen Guiney

I AM the little ass of Christ,
  I carried Him ere He was born,
And bore Him to His bitter Tryst
  Unwilling, that Palm Sunday morn.

I was His Mother's servant, I,
  I carried her from Nazareth,
Up to the shining hill-country
  To see the Lady Elizabeth.

The stones were many in my road,
  By valleys steeper than a cup,
I, trembling for my heavenly load,
  Went cat-foot since I held it up.

To me the wonderful charge was given,
  I, even the little ass, did go
Bearing the very weight of heaven;
  So I crept cat-foot, sure and slow.

Again that night when He was born,
  I carried my dear burdens twain,
And heard dull people's insolent scorn
  Bidding them to the night and rain.

I knelt beside my Brother Ox,
  And saw the very Birth! Oh Love!
And awe and wonder! Little folks
  May see such sights nor die thereof.

The chilly Babe we breathed upon,
  Warmed with our breath the frozen air,
Kneeling beside Our Lady's gown,
  His only comfort saving her.

I am beaten, weary-foot, ill-fed;
  Men curse me: yet I bear withal
Christ's Cross betwixt my shoulders laid,
  So I am honoured, though I'm small.

I served Christ Jesus and I bear
  His cross upon my rough grey back.
Dear Christian people, pray you, spare
  The whip, for Jesus Christ His sake.

THE HAPPY DEAD

To Mary

FOR citizens of God's City
The kind folk have great pity :
  Poor girl, she died a year ago, five years ago.
While blithe ghosts lingering near them
With softest laughter hear them,
  Safe in the bowers of Paradise where roses blow.

The happy souls in heaven,
Washed white as snow new-driven,
  In gardens green, by a clear stream, they walk with
    God.
Withouten grief or sorrow
They wait in hope the morrow.
  To-morrow brings their darlings home by the self-
    same road.

Oh, what friends and what lovers
The newly-come discovers :
  Life of my life, soul of my soul, you come at last!
They shall feed full on kisses,

And more than mortal blisses,
 · The hungry days, the lonely ways, over and past.

Should I go-there before you,
I, your love, who adore you,—
    Let us make tryst : I shall wait for you inside **the**
      gate
That will open to admit you.
How I shall meet you and greet you !
    Heart of my heart, life of my life, you come so late.

The kind folk who are living,
'Tis they have pity and grieving,
    And none will listen to her blame : *Poor girl, she's*
      dead.
Who in the clouds of glory
Knows parting transitory,
    Soul of my soul, oh weep no more : be comforted!

THE WILD PIGEONS

To James Stephens

THE moan of the wild pigeons,
  And the boughs are bare,
Bids my heart remember
  Friends and days that were.

Moan of the wild pigeons
  Sets my heart to weep.
Wakens the grief, the sorrow
  Long had drowsed asleep.

Moan of the wild pigeons,
  North Wind and the snow,
Where the kind ones travelled
  I am fain to go.

They are asleep, the beloved,
  Out in the night and rain.
The moan of the wild pigeons
  Breaks my heart in twain.

AFTER COMMUNION

I CARRY now within my breast
The Son of God ; His rest, His nest :
As Mary's arms once cradled close
Her Rose of Heaven, her golden Rose.

I am the stable and the bed,
The holy hay where He was laid.
The angels stand at gaze to see
What wonder hath been wrought on me.

I am the House of Nazareth,
Where Jesus drew His quiet breath,
When He was little and a boy,
His father's light, His mother's joy.

I am the ass went carrying,
Ere He was born, the Precious Thing ;
The ass, whereof God's guard did keep
The four little feet lest they should slip.

I am the room wherein was set
The Last Supper's most heavenly meat ;
And I the platter and the cup
He gave to them when He did sup.

I am the Cross, whereon He lay,
The rock-hewn grave cold as the clay ;
But not the garden green wherein
He talked with Mary Magdalen.

I shine beyond the fairest star,
More than the constellations are,
A little while : till He is gone,
And all my lights die, one by one.

I am naught but common clay, so hard.
I bring nor balm nor spikenard ;
Nor fling Him Magdalen's beauteous fleece,
Nor shed her tears that win heart's ease.

Yet am His Cup : no porcelain fine,
Nor wrought silver, nor gold ashine :
His choice : and shining by that bliss
Beyond the heavenly chalices.

MENACE

I came into your room and spoke.
  Sudden I knew you were not there.
The easy, common sentence broke
  Against the unanswering air.

My heart shook like a frightened bird,
  And to my ear the terror said,
Where nothing spoke and nothing stirred,
  Dear God, if he were dead!

I heard your footstep in the house,
  Your voice brought comfort to my fear.
But, fluttering like a frightened mouse,
  My heart beat at my ear.

The room wore its familiar face;
  On the warm hearth spirted the flame.
Yet—menace of an empty place—
  Lord, if he never came!

THE VISION

To Miriam Knight

THE village shop's back parlour
   Had curtains snowy white.
The country stretched below it,
   A vision of delight.

Oh, field and farm and coppice
   And shining vale and hill!
Where sang through scented darkness
   The nightingale his fill.

So white it was, the parlour,
   My heart still made its moan
That you and I, oh, dear ones,
   Might have it for our own.

Oh, my tall girl who left me,
   And could you stoop so low,
How I should work to please you,
   And you should sit and sew!

My boy, the world's width from me,
  Should keep the garden trim ;
And never more go straying
  And-take my life with him.

The woman thought me crazy,
  Bereft of sight and speech.
Nor knew my eyes were seeing
  A heaven beyond my reach.

THE ABBOT'S PENANCE

To Father Gilbert Dolan, O.S.B.

FATHER BENNET, who was our Abbot,
Praised God after his habit,
Saw His love in the sun and the dews,
The dusty road and the holes in his shoes.

He thanked Him in fasting and feasting
For the greatest good and also the least thing
The moon and stars, the flowers and fruit,
The rain and wind and a bleeding foot.

He praised Him for health and for sickness,
For the oxen's strength and the lamb her meekness,
For Sleep our sister and Death our brother,
For Toil and Rest and Darkness our mother.

One day as he said, Laudate!
For figs and black bread, one of the Frate,
Vinegar-faced, bade the wine to pass,
Groaning his Deo Gratias.

Good was Brother Leo at fasting,
His Lent was all the year, everlasting.
He ate salt fish with a bitter face
Even on Christmas and Easter Days.

He said his Hours in the grimmest humour;
His ear inclined to tattle and rumour;
While others feasted and praised the Lord
He sat, Death's head at the festal board.

Father Bennet, who oft reproved him
After a merry fashion, yet loved him.
" Pax ! my brother," he said : " Receive
A penance from me that thy soul may live.

Pax, my Leo, who pliest unsparing
Whip and scourge past thy body's bearing.
Beware at the Great Assize to be
Lest that thy body complain of thee.·

God made the body, golden and ruddy ;
He made the soul and He made the body:
Nor would He the soul the body oppress
Over-much for its weaknesses.

I charge thee by our holy obedience
That thy body feast on this dish of pigeons.
Eat of the fruit and drink of the wine
And praise God with the ass and kine.

Praise Him now for His myriad favours,
His kind devising of flavours and savours.
Pax, my brother; now sit and eat
And praise the Giver of wine and meat!"

Fra Leo ate as the meat was bitter—
I have the story from Brother Peter—
Peter our cellarer, palate fine
For the rightful choosing of Capri wine.

Fra Leo ate: and his visage surly
Cleared, as you see it at morning early
When the sun comes out through the shrouding mist
And the hills are roses and amethyst.

As the starved body was warmed and nourished,
The pinched soul that was dry and perished,
Grew, expanded, was kind and throve;
Forsaking sourness it turned to love,

Bennet, our Abbot, his soul's in glory.
He hath joys eternal for transitory.
Leo, Abbot, grown round and kind,
Praises God with an equal mind.

A SONG OF MAY

To George Russell

SPEEDWELL and starwort
  In an English May ;
And to mine own country
  My heart is away.

Sweet was mine own country
  In the days long gone.
Speedwell and starwort,
  Let me alone !

Ground-ivy purple
  In an English furrow.
But my heart's yesterday
  Has no to-morrow.

There is wild forget-me-not
  On the English leas :
My heart is not forgetting
  For those or these.

There is scarlet of poppies
   In the English wheat :
Mother, when I forget thee
   My rest shall be sweet.

My sleep shall be deep,
   I who told thy praises,
In the English clay
   Under English daisies.

When I forget thee,
   Land of desire,
My hands shall be folded
   And my feet not tire.

Speedwell and starwort
   And the wild hedge-rose,
I am not forgetting
   For these or for those.

Poppies and ground-ivy,
   Shall I sleep so sound
That I shall not dream of thee
   In the English ground ?

THE CHILDREN OF HEAVEN

To Nancy Campbell

THE night it was jewelled
   That gave Him birth
With the flight of small angels
   'Twixt heaven and earth.

They were babies rosy,
   Their heads soft-curled,
They came seeking, small roses,
   The Rose of the World.

Like a shower of starshine
   Or broken suns
They were rising and falling
   In millions.

When they came to the stable
   Soft was their flight,
Some Rose Tree in Heaven
   Shook down red and white.

Soft as snows falling
  They settled down,
Clad the poor stable
  In a rosy gown.

Clad the poor stable
  In gold and silk;
Their wings and their shoulders
  Were white as milk.

They peeped at the windows,
  Perched on the wall,
Like birds in the autumn
  When the Southlands call.

And who are these drifting
  As soft as snows,
For little Christ Jesus
  His playfellows ?

They are hiding and peeping,
  Rosy and pale,
From the stable's shadows
  And His Mother's veil.

They are pushing and pressing
 By the window-sill;
Between their wing feathers
 They look their fill.

There's a rustling, a stealing
 Of feet and wings.
Perched on the manger
 One softly sings.

Come nearer, children,
 And see Him lie
On the knees of His Mother
 So quietly !

Come all, ye children,
 Nor fear the while
The frown of His Mother;
 Nay,—see her smile !

The flight of child-angels
 When He was born
Made the morn of Christmas
 A rosy morn.

THANKSGIVING

To May Sinclair

I THANK God when I kneel to pray
That mine is still the middle way,

Set in a safe and sweet estate
Between the little and the great ;

Not troubled with wealth's cares nor yet
Too poor where needs that cark and fret

Push out sweet leisure and green nooks,
And give no chance for talk and books.

I take my middle way between
The mansion and a lodging mean.

My cottage at the country's edge
Hath sweetbriar growing in its hedge,

Honesty, heartsease and sweet-peas,
Herb-bennet, love-in-idleness.

Give me a tree, a well, a hive,
And I can save my soul alive,

Yet be as poor in spirit as
The Poverello's Lady was.

I covet not soft silk or lace
Nor any lovely lady's face ;

Nor yet would go in hodden grey ;
But lawns and wool be my array.

I still may ask a friend to dine
And set him meat and pour him wine;

Nor count the coins within my purse
To see that I am nothing worse.

I thank God that my middle place
Is set amid much pleasantness.

And not too high and not too low
The safe, untroubled path I go.

LIGHT

To Padraic Colum

As I looked o'er Killiney to the Golden Spears
The light on the water was there as in old years,
The light on the water I never saw elsewhere.
It set 'twixt sea and heaven a jewelled stair,
Á stair into heaven : and I said in my mind
God's Eyes o'er Killiney looked down and were kind.

As I looked from Killiney away to Wicklow Hill
The light on the headlands kept rising, falling still :
All set with fine jewels, a halo for God's hair ;
The light over Wicklow a cloak for Him to wear.
I knew that in heaven He smiled and was glad
For the beauty of His handiwork, the thing He made.

As I looked from Killiney o'er the vales below,
A cloud as smoke hung steady till the wind should blow.
And from its lustrous curtain like the Temple veil
Five streams of light down-pouring lit hill and vale.
God raised His hand for blessing in the cloud's eclipse,
Shed the light and the glory from His finger-tips.

THE CHRISTENING

O CALL the child from some kind saint
  So quick to run and save,
Not Deirdre with the griefs acquaint,
  Not Grania nor Maeve.

Not Daphne, Phœbe, Phyllis, Prue,
  Nor any country Grace,
Lest that your gossips prove untrue
  In some most bitter case.

In heaven there stand, carnations fair
  Beside our dear Lord's knee.
Margaret, Catherine, Magdalen, Clare,
  Dorothy, Cecily.

And all day long in the still place
  Their haloes fall and rise,
Their faces turned to the one Face,
  The glory on their eyes.

Or give the chrisomed child to keep
  To Mary of the Swords:
The heart that held God's Son asleep
  Is soft to babes and birds.

The world is set with many a snare
  Where evil things affright.
Give her a name that she may wear
  Like armour in God's sight.

Give to her little stumbling feet
  A help most sure and kind,
That when she cries a foot so fleet
  Run to her like the wind.

Give her a name that frights God's foes,
  The name one bears who is
In God's rose-garden a tall rose
  Among the white lilies.

Give her a friend who will not fail,
  Who walks in white so brave.
Not Deirdre of the Sorrows pale
  Nor Grania, nor Maeve.

THE NIGHT COMETH

DEEPER and deeper grows the shade,
　　It will be dark ere evening come ;
Yet shall my heart be not dismayed
　　If Thou art with me in the gloom.

What though the faces grow more dim,
　　The kind and friendly faces all,
If Thou, girt by the Cherubim,
　　Should'st walk with me at evenfall ?

What though Thy hills die off in mist,
　　Thy sky, Thy stars, Thy night, Thy morn—
Though grey be rose and amethyst
　　And of earth's glory I am shorn ?

What if Thy face should rise upon
　　·My starless night and I should see
Its beauty more than moon and sun
　　Lighting my darkness wonderfully ?

What if this beauteous world Thou'st wrought
  Were but a maze where I should stray
And lose Thee,—losing Thee have naught!
  Let night fall on Thy world and day?

Oh, if in clouds of blackest night
  Groping I find Thy fingers kind,
Thine eyes turn all my darkness light:
  Star of my blindness, be I blind!

THE PARABLE OF THE RICH MAN

To Mr. Justice Gibson

LORD JESUS stood at Paradise gate
  And saw a myriad worlds and stars.
Oh what is this so desolate
  Clinging to the gold bars ?

The salt spume on its eyes and lips,
  The seaweed tangled in its hair.
Oh, scourged with bitter thorns and whips,
  What seas have stripped thee bare ?

Lord Jesus bowed His comely head
  With : "What art thou, thou thing forlorn ?"
"Oh, I am a rich man's soul," it said,
  "That died ere I was born.

By Thine own lips was judgment given,
  Yea, judgment sharper than a sword.
How shall a rich man enter heaven ?
  Yea, Thou hast said it, Lord."

It was the dead oped lips to cry
  "How should I save my soul, alas !
Since easier through the needle's eye
  The camel's shape should pass ? "

Lord Jesus, Who hath ruth for all,
  Had pity on the rich man's doom :
" I can do all things great and small,
  Yea, give the camel room.

But who is it has hurt thee, say :
  Made thee one gaping wound and marred
Out of immortal likeness, yea
  As I was, marred and scarred ? "

" And knowest Thou not, Lord Christ, this hour,
  Who knowest all has been, shall be,
That the great ship, new Babel's Tower,
  Is sunk beneath the sea ?

The iceberg pierced her monstrous side,
  As frail as any cockle-shell :
With a great sob she plunged and died.
  Oh, Lord, what need of hell ?

The rich men now that went so brave
  Drift 'twixt Cape Race and Labrador.
Not such as these Thou diedst to save,
  Thou Saviour of the poor.

Not these, not these, Thou diedst to win.
  Thy Passion was not spent for them.
Have I not purged me from my sin
  Who heard the women scream ? ''

" Son,—I was there and saw thee die.
  The unstable waters bore Me up,
Whose hollowed hand can hold the sky,
  Sun, stars, as in a cup.

I, Shepherd of the Ocean, passed,
  Gathered My lambs, gathered My sheep ;
Saw rich men greatly die at last.
  Yea, what they lost they keep.

That was the door I openéd,
  Narrow and high in Paradise wall,
That they should die in another's stead
  For Mine, the meek and small.

That which they cast away they save.
   They paid their debt in full.   One breath,
Smiled on the innumerable grave,
   Leaped, and found Life, not Death.

Not through the needle's eye may fare
   The camel : by a straiter gate
Naked and scourged, made clean and bare,
   The rich man enters late."

GORSE

To W. B. Yeats, who taught me

MANY a year I loved the gorse on an English common,
   Miles on miles of the golden cups and the nutty wine,
Cloth of gold for the tramping folk, poor men and
      women ;
   Still my heart said in complaint : It is not mine.

Here's a golden wall each side the hill we're breasting ;
   Never sure was the English gorse as great as this !
Grapes of gold from a golden vine for the wild bees'
      questing ;
   A world of gold and a pearly cloud on a blue abyss.

There's a golden hill behind us now, gold on the azure,
   The dearest hill like a little breast in gold above.
The lark springs from a golden bed, spilling his treasure
   Down on the buttercup fields of light and his hidden
      love.

Over the hill we bathe our feet in golden water,
   A little stream the traveller fords, so clear and cold.

But is it May of the leafing—the High King's daughter
  For all her green is under the wave of the flooding
    gold.

Over the hill—the yellow hill, the Spears are showing,
  The Silver Spears are turned to gold o'er the valley's
    haze.
There's a small gold shower on the mountain now and
    the river flowing
  Flows in and out like a ribbon of gold through the
    Milky Ways.

The eager bees plunge to the thighs in a brimming
    chalice,
  Their bag so full of the golden spoils they scarce can
    fly—
The mountain calls to the mountain now, over the valleys,
  " Friend, we are Kings in the house of Kings, you
    and I."

Here with a heart fed of delight as a bee with honey
  I sit like a miser counting the gold, nor shall repine,
For the cuckoo's roaming the golden street, blithesome
    and bonny—
  My heart says to my heart: Have peace: this
    beauty's thine.

G. W.

(*June 8th*, 1913)

SOLDIER, poet, courtier,
　He was these and more than these.
He must go to find his peer,
　Over mountains, over seas,
To some starry world afar
Where the constellations are.

Traveller from the realms of gold,
　Sidney's brother, Raleigh's twin,
From this cynic world and old
　Some strange jest hath placed him in,
Eldorado and the morn
Unto these he shall return.

Whither goest, adventurer,
　With the East upon thine eyes,
Stepping with the old blithesome air
　On the last splendid enterprise ?
Who hast heard the piper play
Over the hills and far away.

Dear Prince Charming, fair and young,
   'Scaped from sickness and sad age,
Take a blessing and a song
   When thou goest on pilgrimage,
Where the lark goes, high, on high,
The white road thou travellest by.

PRINTED BY
HAZELL, WATSON AND VINEY, LD.,
LONDON AND AYLESBURY.

CPSIA information can be obtained
at www.ICGtesting.com
Printed in the USA
BVHW08s1237060818
523682BV00023B/1113/P